LAUREL COUNTY PUBLIC LIBRARY

D0919103

Level 2,3
0,5

Sea Otters

by Anne Wendorff

BELLWETHER MEDIA · MINNEAPOLIS, MN

BLASTOFF!
2
READERS

Note to Librarians, Teachers, and Parents:

Blastoff! Readers are carefully developed by literacy experts and combine standards-based content with developmentally appropriate text.

Level 1 provides the most support through repetition of high-frequency words, light text, predictable sentence patterns, and strong visual support.

Level 2 offers early readers a bit more challenge through varied simple sentences, increased text load, and less repetition of high-frequency words.

Level 3 advances early-fluent readers toward fluency through increased text and concept load, less reliance on visuals, longer sentences, and more literary language.

Level 4 builds reading stamina by providing more text per page, increased use of punctuation, greater variation in sentence patterns, and increasingly challenging vocabulary.

Level 5 encourages children to move from "learning to read" to "reading to learn" by providing even more text, varied writing styles, and less familiar topics.

Whichever book is right for your reader, Blastoff! Readers are the perfect books to build confidence and encourage a love of reading that will last a lifetime!

This edition first published in 2009 by Bellwether Media.

No part of this publication may be reproduced in whole or in part without written permission of the publisher. For information regarding permission, write to Bellwether Media Inc., Attention: Permissions Department, Post Office Box 19349, Minneapolis, MN 55419.

Library of Congress Cataloging-in-Publication Data
Wendorff, Anne.
  Sea otters / by Anne Wendorff.
     p. cm. – (Blastoff! readers. Oceans alive)
  Summary: "Simple text and full color photographs introduce beginning readers to sea otters. Developed by literacy experts for students in kindergarten through third grade"—Provided by publisher.
  Includes bibliographical references and index.
  ISBN-13: 978-1-60014-207-9 (hardcover : alk. paper)
  ISBN-10: 1-60014-207-9 (hardcover : alk. paper)
  1. Sea otter—Juvenile literature. I. Title.

  QL737.C25W46 2009
  599.769'5–dc22   2008017348

Text copyright © 2009 by Bellwether Media Inc. BLASTOFF! READERS and associated logos are trademarks and/or registered trademarks of Bellwether Media Inc.

SCHOLASTIC, CHILDREN'S PRESS, and associated logos are trademarks and/or registered trademarks of Scholastic Inc. Printed in the United States of America.

Contents

Sea otters are small
ocean **mammals**.

Sea otters are **warm-blooded**.
They live in the Pacific Ocean.

Sea otters have two layers of fur. One layer is short and one layer is long.

The two layers of fur
keep sea otters warm
and dry in cold water.

Sea otters have **webbed feet** and a flat tail. These help them swim fast.

Sea otters live around **kelp beds**. Kelp is a kind of seaweed.

Sea otters must swim fast to escape from sharks, whales, and other **predators**.

9

whiskers

Sea otters have **whiskers**.

Whiskers help them f
food in dark water.

Kelp beds are home to
many animals sea otters
like to eat.

Sea otters dive into kelp
beds to hunt for food.

They look for fish, crabs, snails, and **sea urchins**.

Sea otters use rocks to break open the shells of **prey**.

Sea otters float on their backs while they eat.

Sea otters eat and live in groups called **rafts**.

Rafts of sea otters float
on their backs together.

They wrap themselves in kelp
to keep from floating away.

Sea otters eat, sleep, and play together in the ocean.

Glossary

kelp bed—an area filled with a kind of seaweed called kelp that is home to many ocean animals

mammal—a warm-blooded animal with a backbone that feeds milk to its young

predator—an animal that hunts other animals for food

prey—an animal hunted by another animal for food

raft—a group of sea otters that live together

sea urchin—an ocean animal that lives inside of a spiny shell

warm-blooded—having a body temperature that is warm and constant

webbed feet—feet with toes connected by skin

whiskers—thick, strong hairs on an animal's face used to feel things

To Learn More

AT THE LIBRARY

Leardi, Jeanette. *Southern Sea Otters: Fur-Tastrophe Avoided.* New York: Bearport, 2007.

Lockwood, Sophie. *Sea Otters.* Chanhassen, Minn.: The Child's World, 2006.

Smith, Roland. *Sea Otter Rescue.* New York: Puffin, 1999.

ON THE WEB

Learning more about sea otters is as easy as 1, 2, 3.

1. Go to www.factsurfer.com

2. Enter "sea otters" into search box.

3. Click the "Surf" button and you will see a list of related web sites.

With factsurfer.com, finding more information is just a click away.

Index

The images in this book are reproduced through the courtesy of: Kevin Schafer / Getty Images, front cover; James D. Watt / Image Quest 3-D, pp. 4-5; Peter Mc Convill / Alamy, p. 6; Gerald & Buff Corsi / Getty Images, p.7; Blaine Harrington III / Alamy, p. 8; Masa Ushioda / Alamy, p. 9; TimFitzharris / Getty Images, pp. 10-11; Jeff Foott / Getty Images, pp. 12-13, 14-15, 20; Norbert Wu / Getty Images, pp. 16-17; Mark Newman / agefotostock, pp. 18-19; Davo Blair / Alamy, p. 21.